Greatnes...

King Spider

Illustrated by
Tinny Rosser

Series Editor: Karen Morrison

About the Author

Greatness Ditlhokwa was born and grew up in Botswana. He trained as an art teacher, and has also studied videography. Now living and working in Gaborone, he is an artist, photographer and cartoonist as well as a writer.

Heinemann Educational Publishers
Halley Court, Jordan Hill, Oxford OX2 8EJ
A division of Reed Educational & Professional Publishing Ltd

Heinemann Educational Books (Nigeria) Ltd
PMB 5205, Ibadan
Heinemann Educational Botswana Publishers (Pty) Ltd
PO Box 10103, Village Post Office, Gaborone, Botswana

FLORENCE PRAGUE MADRID ATHENS
MELBOURNE AUCKLAND TOKYO SINGAPORE KUALA LUMPUR
PORTSMOUTH NH (USA) MEXICO CITY CHICAGO
SAO PAULO JOHANNESBURG KAMPALA NAIROBI

© Greatness Ditlhokwa 1996
First published by Heinemann Educational Publishers in 1996
The right of Greatness Ditlhokwa to be identified as the author of this work has been asserted by him in accordance with the Copyright, Designs and Patents Act 1988

British Library Cataloguing in Publication Data
A catalogue record for this book is available
from the British Library

ISBN 0 435 89120 0

Glossary
Difficult words are listed alphabetically on page 29

Edited by Christine King
Designed by The Point
Printed and bound by George Over Ltd, Rugby and London

96 97 98 99 10 9 8 7 6 5 4 3 2 1

Long, long ago in the very beginning of the world, all living creatures could talk like people do today.

Lion was the king of all the beasts. But he didn't pay much attention to the millions of small crawling and flying beasts in his kingdom.

Spider decided that the smaller beasts needed their own king. So he took it upon himself to rule over them.

He called a big meeting and told the small beasts, 'I have been chosen to be your king!'

The small beasts thought that Lion had chosen Spider to be king. They all applauded loudly. They were happy to have a king of their own.

'I will represent you at Lion's big meetings,' announced Spider.

The small creatures applauded again – they were happy to miss boring old meetings!

However, Spider turned into a very bossy and lazy king.

He made the ants, bees, crickets, butterflies, scorpions and other crawling and flying beasts work for him.

Spider himself sat in a tree and shouted orders.

'Get me food! Get me drink!'

Soon, he was very unpopular.

Sometimes Spider went to the big meetings of all creatures. This made him feel important. It also gave him a chance to speak for the small beasts.

After these meetings, he would call the small beasts together and tell them what Lion had decided. For this reason, the small beasts tolerated Spider as their king.

One day, when the sun was very hot, Spider called a meeting of all the small beasts.

But they were all resting in shady places. Scorpions were hiding under rocks. Butterflies and bees were resting in leafy plants. Even the hard-working ants were staying in the shade.

So nobody attended the meeting.

Spider waited and waited. The sun rose higher and higher and it got hotter and hotter. Still no one came.

When Spider realised that the beasts were not coming, he got very angry. He made a huge fire from green leaves and branches. The smoke spread over the land, awakening all the small beasts that were in its reach.

The small beasts were very unhappy with Spider. They were hot and tired and they wanted to sleep peacefully in the shade. They were also tired of Spider's meetings.

However, they were also a bit scared of Spider, so they decided to drag themselves to the meeting.

The smoke from the fire made them cough. But they slowly made their way to Spider's place.

The small beasts settled on rocks, branches, leaves and grass. They tried hard to stay in the shade, and soon there was no place left to settle. Suddenly Spider sprang from a tree branch and greeted them loudly.

'My friends, I am very worried about your failure to come to meetings on time,' said Spider. 'I know that it is very hot, but I have a plan. I think we should build a big shelter. It will keep us cool, and we can sleep there when the rains come.'

The small beasts knew that this meant work for them and they sighed.

Spider took no notice of their sighing. He explained how and where the shelter should be built. As usual, he expected the others to do all the hard work. Spider himself would be the supervisor.

The small beasts just looked at each other and shook their heads.

When he had finished speaking, Spider waited for applause.

There wasn't any. All the creatures just stared at him.

Spider began to feel uncomfortable.

Then Scorpion stood up and said, 'I wish to say something.'

Spider was glad the silence was broken.

Scorpion looked around at the creatures and said, 'Our king has a very good plan, but there is a problem. How can we build a shelter for all of us when we are all different? Some of us like to live on the ground, others like trees and some even like to live in water.'

The small beasts were nodding in agreement. Scorpion went on, 'I think we shall have to build ourselves individual shelters.'

His audience applauded. 'That's a good idea,' they all said.

Soon there was a loud buzzing. Scorpion's idea had excited the small beasts and they immediately began to make plans.

Spider looked at them. He did not know what to say. He did not want to build his own shelter because he was far too lazy. He tried to speak but the other creatures were busy discussing their shelters.

Spider jumped up and down with anger. Then the others did notice and grew quiet.

'Scorpion has a very good idea,' said Spider. 'But the custom of our land is that the king comes first. You must first build a shelter for me.'

The other creatures were silent. They did not want to build a shelter for Spider.

'Off you go to collect fine materials for my new shelter,' commanded Spider.

The other creatures went away muttering to themselves. As they walked away, Scorpion gathered them into small groups and whispered to them.

Spider climbed to the top of a tall tree and watched the insects collecting building material.

The ants dragged leaves and twigs. The wasps carried mud and leaves. The grasshoppers dug holes in the ground. Scorpion was nowhere to be seen.

Spider felt pleased when he saw everyone so busy. He dreamed of his wonderful shelter. He pictured large rooms for him to sleep in and a huge store-room for food.

'Later,' he said to himself, 'I shall make them fill my store-room with food.'

Spider watched and waited patiently, but nobody returned with material for his shelter.

Soon Spider realised that they were not going to build him a shelter. He flew into a rage and began to jump up and down on his eight legs, shouting at the other beasts and cursing them.

While Spider was jumping up and down and deciding how to punish his disloyal subjects, it began to rain. And still Spider had no shelter!

All the others ran to the shelters they had built. Spider hid beneath some leaves. He was very wet, very angry and very miserable.

The rain went on for a whole month. When it stopped, Spider decided he was going to punish the insects for failing him.

But he could not find them. They were all safe in their shelters.

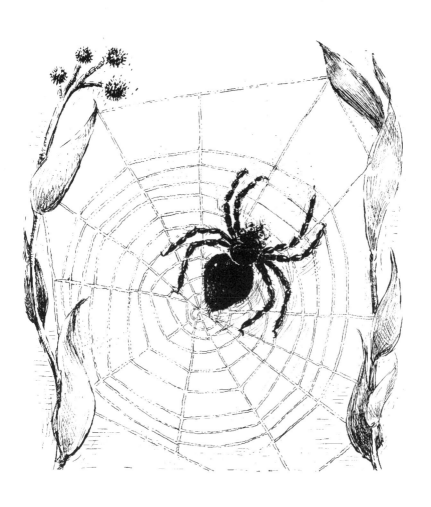

Then Spider made another plan.
He squeezed sticky threads of silk from his body and used them to weave a large web between the branches of a tree. Then he sat down to wait.

He did not have to wait long. Soon an insect came flying past. It did not even see the web, and in seconds it was trapped in the sticky threads.

Spider came over and wrapped it up with more thread so that it could not escape.

Within a day or two, Spider had so many insects tied up that the web was full. He knew he had taught the insects a lesson, but he did not know what to do with the ones he had trapped.

Spider left them in the web and sat down to think.

Soon Spider felt hungry. He looked around for something to eat. But there was nothing except the insects in his web.

'Hmmm,' he thought. 'I wonder what they'll taste like.'

He bit a hole in the silk threads round one insect and slowly sucked out its juices. The insect tasted so good that Spider ate a few more.

Spider only stopped eating insects when he was really full. Then he sat back and laughed.

'I may not be king now,' he said, 'but the insects will still supply me with food after all!'

Questions

1 Who made Spider king of the small beasts?
2 Why was Spider an unpopular king?
3 What was Spider's big idea?
4 What did Scorpion suggest at the meeting?
5 Who did the small beasts listen to – Spider or Scorpion?
6 What did the small beasts use to make their shelters?
7 Where was Spider when it began to rain?
8 When did Spider decide to punish the others?
9 How did he punish them?

Activities

1 Bees, ants, wasps and scorpions are all small beasts. Write down the names of some other small beasts that you find in your area.
2 The spider in the story is big and hairy. Draw a different spider that you have seen. Try to find out its name.
3 Find out some other ways in which spiders catch insects.

Glossary

applauded (page 3) clapped, to show agreement

commanded (page 17) ordered to do something

cursing (page 20) calling for evil things to happen

custom (page 16) the usual way of doing things

disloyal (page 21) not being true to someone

individual (page 14) for one person

muttering (page 17) speaking softly under one's breath

represent (page 3) act for them

supervisor (page 11) a person who checks that work is done

tolerated (page 5) put up with him: allowed him to continue even though they didn't entirely agree with him

The Junior African Writers Series is designed to provide interesting and varied African stories both for pleasure and for study. There are five graded levels in the series.

Level 1 is for readers who have been studying English for three to four years. The content and language have been carefully controlled to increase fluency in reading.

Content The plots are simple and the number of characters is kept to a minimum. The information is presented in small manageable amounts and the illustrations reinforce the text.

Language Reading is a learning experience and, although the choice of words is carefully controlled, new words, important to the story, are also introduced. These are contextualised and explained in the glossary.

Glossary Difficult words which learners may not know have been listed alphabetically at the end of the book. The definitions refer to the way the word is used in the story, and the page reference is for the word's first use.

Questions and **Activities** The questions give useful comprehension practice and ensure that the reader has followed and understood the story. The activities develop themes and ideas introduced, and can be done as pairwork or groupwork in class, or as homework.

JAWS Starters

In addition to the five levels of JAWS titles, there are three levels of JAWS Starters. These are full-colour picture books designed to lead in to the first level of JAWS.